★ ★ ★ ★ ★ MILITARY FAM

My Sister Is in the
COAST GUARD

VINCE TOTH

PowerKiDS press.

New York

Published in 2016 by The Rosen Publishing Group, Inc.
29 East 21st Street, New York, NY 10010

First Edition

Editor: Sarah Machajewski
Book Design: Katelyn Heinle/Reann Nye

Photo Credits: Cover, pp. 5, 7 (top), 9 (bottom), 11, 13 (bottom), 17 (both), 19 (both), 22 (soldier) courtesy of U.S. Coast Guard Flickr; cover backdrop, p. 1 David Smart/Shutterstock.com; pp. 3–4, 6, 8, 10, 12, 14, 16, 18, 20, 22, 24 (camouflage texture) Casper1774/Shutterstock.com; p. 7 (bottom) Dragon Images/Shutterstock.com; p. 9 (top) Archive Holdings Inc./The Image Bank/Getty Images; p. 13 (map) ekler/Shutterstock.com; p. 15 (top) courtesy Petty Officer 2nd Class Patrick Kelley/Defense Video & Imagery Distribution System; p. 15 (bottom) courtesy Petty Officer 1st Class Nick Ameen/Defense Video & Imagery Distribution System; p. 21 Joe Raedle/Getty Images North America/Getty Images; p. 22 (American flag) Naypong/Shutterstock.com.

Library of Congress Cataloging-in-Publication Data

Toth, Vince, author.
  My sister is in the Coast Guard / Vince Toth.
      pages cm. — (Military families)
  Includes index.
  ISBN 978-1-5081-4442-7 (pbk.)
  ISBN 978-1-5081-4443-4 (6 pack)
  ISBN 978-1-5081-4444-1 (library binding)
  1. United States. Coast Guard—Juvenile literature. I. Title.
  VG53.T67 2016
  363.28'60973—dc23
                                    2015034620

Manufactured in the United States of America

CPSIA Compliance Information: Batch #BW16PK: For Further Information contact Rosen Publishing, New York, New York at 1-800-237-9932

CONTENTS

Meet My Sister

The United States has one of the largest militaries in the world. As of 2015, more than 2 million people serve in the military. My sister is one of them. She serves in the United States Coast Guard. The coast guard **protects** our country and keeps its citizens safe. As a coastguardsman, my sister helps carry out this duty.

My sister joined the coast guard a few years ago. Her life has changed a lot since then. My family's life changed, too. My sister's job isn't always easy, but it's very important. I look up to my sister a lot.

★★★
Military Matters
Men and women who serve in the coast guard are called coastguardsmen.

MY SISTER IS MY BEST FRIEND, A COASTGUARDSMAN,
AND MY HERO.

A Look at the Military

The U.S. military has five branches. Each branch does something different. The coast guard mostly works on **missions** that are carried out on water, such as rivers, ports, and coasts. The other branches are the army, navy, Marine **Corps**, and air force. These branches take care of missions on land, in the air, and at sea.

The coast guard is one of the smallest military branches. It's made of active-duty coastguardsmen and reserve coastguardsmen. My sister is an active-duty coastguardsman. If she wanted to serve in the coast guard and have another job, she could have joined the Coast Guard Reserve.

★ ★ ★

Military Matters

The Coast Guard Reserve is a group of coastguardsmen who are called on to serve in times of need.

ACTIVE-DUTY
COASTGUARDSMAN

RESERVE
COASTGUARDSMAN

"ACTIVE DUTY" MEANS A PERSON WORKS FOR THE COAST GUARD FULL TIME. RESERVE COASTGUARDSMEN WORK FOR THE COAST GUARD PART TIME. THEY OFTEN HAVE OTHER JOBS, TOO.

The History of the Coast Guard

The U.S. Coast Guard formed shortly after the United States became a country. In 1790, George Washington signed an act that called for 10 **vessels** to **enforce** tax and trade laws, as well as to keep **smuggling** from happening. In 1915, this group officially became the coast guard.

In 2003, the coast guard became part of the Department of **Homeland Security**. As part of this group, the coast guard protects the United States during times of peace and war. It guards U.S. ports and keeps our waterways safe. The coast guard also enforces U.S. laws at sea and performs search-and-rescue missions. These are just some responsibilities my sister has.

THE COAST GUARD WORKS HARD TO KEEP THE UNITED STATES SAFE. IN 2012, IT HANDLED MORE THAN 20,000 SEARCH-AND-RESCUE CASES AND SEARCHED ABOUT 1,700 BOATS THAT WERE TRAVELING TO THE UNITED STATES.

1945

2015

SIGNING UP

What does it take to join the coast guard? People who **enlist** for active duty have to be between 17 and 27. Future coastguardsmen must complete a high school education, and they must pass a background check. A background check is something that tells if someone has committed a crime.

It's important for coastguardsmen to be healthy, so everyone has to pass a health exam. They also have to pass an ASVAB test. This test helps people who enlist figure out what their career with the coast guard will be. My sister was able to enlist because she met all these requirements.

Since they spend a lot of time on and in the water, coastguardsmen must be good swimmers. Being healthy and strong is important!

Training to Be the Best

All coast guard **recruits** go to basic training after they enlist. My sister had to leave home for training. Coast guard training takes place in Cape May, New Jersey. It's far from home, and I missed my sister a lot when she left.

My sister told me all about basic training. On her first day, she met her **company** commander, or CC. The CC led my sister and other recruits through training. They learned the skills they needed to be in the coast guard, such as safety, firefighting skills, how to rescue people, and how to use **weapons**. My sister also learned how to work as part of a team.

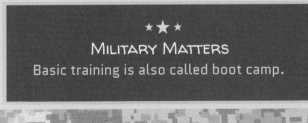

★★★
Military Matters
Basic training is also called boot camp.

CAPE MAY,
NEW JERSEY

UNITED STATES

MY SISTER SAID HER CC WAS LIKE A COACH OR TEACHER. THE CC TAUGHT HER AND OTHER RECRUITS ABOUT **DISCIPLINE** AND HOW TO FOLLOW ORDERS.

Coast guard boot camp lasts for eight weeks. My sister said she was busy every day during training. During the fourth week, my sister picked where she wanted work after training. She also got to pick if she wanted to work ashore, which means on land, or afloat, which means on water.

My family couldn't talk to my sister during training, but we wrote her letters every night. We finally got to see her when she graduated from training. Coastguardsmen graduate as either seamen or firemen. My sister graduated as a seaman. My family is really proud of her! She's proud of herself, too.

Families travel to Cape May every year to see their family member graduate from training. It's often the first time in weeks they've seen their coastguardsman!

Coast Guard Careers

After boot camp, my sister went to more training for her career. My sister is a boatswain's mate. Her job is really cool. She gets to drive cutters, which is what the coast guard calls its boats. My sister operates and takes care of the **equipment** on the cutters. She gets to do search-and-rescue missions. My sister says her most important job is enforcing laws and protecting our country's waterways.

My sister's career is just one of many the coast guard offers. The coast guard has electricians, **intelligence** specialists, health-care workers, and more.

MY SISTER KNOWS HOW TO DRIVE CUTTERS JUST LIKE THIS ONE. IT'S A LOT OF RESPONSIBILITY.

What's It Like for My Sister?

My sister knew her life would change after joining the coast guard. She had to move away from home for training and then move somewhere else for her job. It was hard for her to leave our family, but she knows we support her.

My sister joined the coast guard because she wanted to serve her country. The coast guard is always on duty, so my sister has to be ready to work when she's needed. And she has to go where the coast guard tells her. This includes moving to a new place if the coast guard needs her there.

MY SISTER'S JOB CAN SOMETIMES BE DANGEROUS, OR UNSAFE. COASTGUARDSMEN HAVE TO RESCUE PEOPLE WHO ARE IN TROUBLE IN THE WATER AND DEAL WITH PEOPLE WHO BREAK THE LAW. COASTGUARDSMEN ARE VERY BRAVE.

WHAT'S IT LIKE FOR MY FAMILY?

It was a big deal when my sister joined the coast guard. My family felt very proud of her, but we were sad she had to leave home. I miss my sister a lot, but I talk to her every day. We can talk on the phone or over the computer. She's able to come home to visit, too.

One thing that's hard about having a sister in the coast guard is that she can be deployed one day. That means the coast guard can send her overseas on a mission. My sister is brave and says she would be proud to serve her country this way.

IF YOU HAVE A FAMILY MEMBER WHO'S DEPLOYED, YOU KNOW IT CAN BE HARD. IT'S OK TO BE SAD, MAD, OR WORRIED UNTIL YOUR FAMILY MEMBER COMES HOME. IT CAN HELP TO TALK TO A TRUSTED ADULT ABOUT HOW YOU FEEL.

Supporting Our Heroes

Life with the coast guard is very exciting. My sister gets to protect our country at home. Some coastguardsmen protect the United States overseas. My sister gets to carry out the law, keep people safe, and help people in need. Her job is very important!

One thing I've learned from having a family member in the military is that my family's support is really important. Servicemen and servicewomen make a lot of **sacrifices** to keep us safe. Our support and pride are things that help them do their job. The people in our country's military—especially my sister—are my heroes!

Glossary

company: A group within a military branch.

corps: A group within a branch of a military organization that does a particular kind of work.

discipline: Controlled behavior.

enforce: To carry out.

enlist: To join.

equipment: The objects needed for a certain purpose.

homeland security: A term that's used for the U.S. government's efforts to keep the United States safe from enemies.

intelligence: Information that is of military or political value.

mission: An important job.

protect: To keep safe.

recruit: A person new to the armed forces who is not yet fully trained.

sacrifice: Something given up for a larger purpose.

smuggle: To move goods into or out of a country illegally.

vessel: A ship or large boat.

weapon: Something used to cause harm.

Index

Websites

Due to the changing nature of Internet links, PowerKids Press has developed an online list of websites related to the subject of this book. This site is updated regularly. Please use this link to access the list: www.powerkidslinks.com/mili/cstg